A STAR IS BORN

MUSIC FROM THE ORIGINAL MOTION
PICTURE SOUNDTRACK

Produced by
Alfred Music
P.O. Box 10003
Van Nuys, CA 91410-0003
alfred.com

Printed in USA.

ISBN-10: 1-4706-4153-4
ISBN-13: 978-1-4706-4153-5

"Out of Time" is not included in this collection.

BLACK EYES

Words and Music
BRADLEY COOPER and LUKAS NELSON

Optional 8vb throughout

Black Eyes - 6 - 1

8

Guitar Solo:

(Guitar solo ad lib.)

Play 4 times

By the way - side.   I'm by the way - side.

mp

— I'm by the way - side.   Too far__ gone,

Black Eyes - 6 - 3

Bridge:

10

By the way - side._____   By the way - side.

By the way - side.

Verse 2:

Black eyes o - pen wide,___ it's time to tes - ti - fy.___

There's no room___ for lies.___ And ev - 'ry-one's wait - ing for you.

LA VIE EN ROSE

Original French Lyrics by
EDITH PIAF

Music by
LUIS GUGLIELM

14

La Vie en Rose - 4 - 3

15

MAYBE IT'S TIME

Words and Music b[y]
JASON ISBELL

in the things they heard and the things they read.___
in' down___ and laugh - in' at___ our ways.___

No-bod-y knows___ what a - waits_ for___ the dead.___
No-bod-y speaks___ to God_ these___ days.___

I'm

Bridge:

glad I can't go back___ to where_ I came___ from.
When I was a child,___ they tried_ to fool___ me.

I'm glad those days are gone,___ gone for good.
Said the world - ly man was lost___ and that a Hell was real.___

ALIBI

Gtr. tuned Double-Drop D:
⑥ = D ③ = G
⑤ = A ② = B
④ = D ① = D

Words and Music by
LADY GAGA, BRADLEY COOPER
and LUKAS NELSON

Moderate rock ♩ = 89

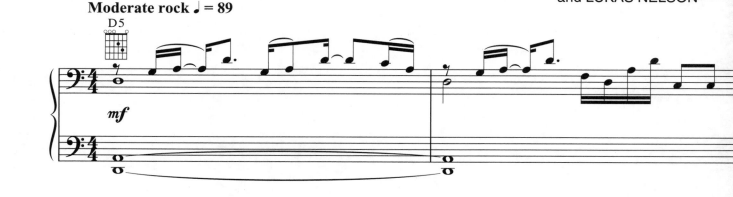

1. Don't

Alibi - 4 - 1

Verse 1:

ask me 'bout to - mor - row, or tell me 'bout my past. My heart is yours to bor - row, ain't

noth-in' meant_ to last.___ I ain't ly - in', I don't lie with-out an al - i - bi._

2. Don't

Verses 2 & 3:

ask too man-y ques-tions you don't want an-swers to. You don't like my di - rec - tion, hell,
love you in the morn-in' and when the day is done. But if you want my free-dom, you

24

I won't fol - low you.___ } I ain't ly - in', I don't lie with-out an al - i - bi.__
know I'm bound_ to run.__

Chorus:

_____ I told my dy-in' dad-dy that I

had to run a - way.___ Looked him in the eye,__ said there

ain't no oth - er way.__ So, wom-an, if I tell__ you that I love_

SHALLOW

Words and Music by
LADY GAGA, MARK RONSON,
ANTHONY ROSSOMANDO and ANDREW WYATT

Shallow - 6 - 1

28

Chorus 3:

MUSIC TO MY EYES

Words and Music by
LADY GAGA and LUKAS NELSON

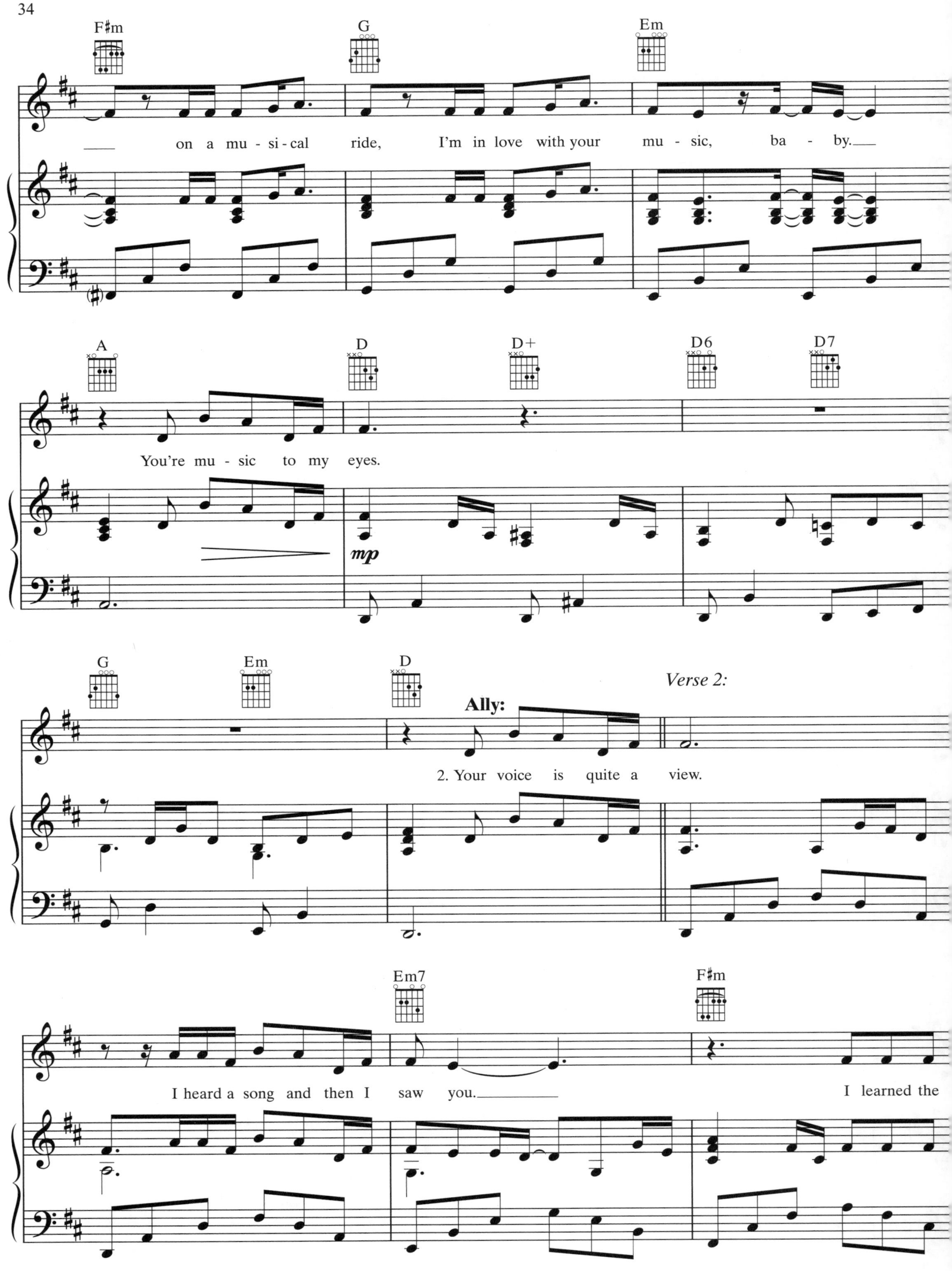

F♯m G Em
on a mu - si - cal ride, I'm in love with your mu - sic, ba - by.
A D D+ D6 D7
You're mu - sic to my eyes.
mp
G Em D
Verse 2:
Ally:
2. Your voice is quite a view.
Em7 F♯m
I heard a song and then I saw you.
I learned the

DIGGIN' MY GRAVE

Words and Music by
PAUL KENNERLEY

Verse 1:

Jackson:

1. You're kill-in' me, ba - by, with the things you do.___

Put me in the ground be - fore___ we're through.___

gin' My Grave - 7 - 1

40

D.S % al Coda

 Coda

You've been out all_____ night

dig-gin' my grave.

Dig-gin' my, dig-gin' my, dig-gin' my, dig-gin' my, dig-gin' my, dig-gin' my,

dig-gin' my, dig-gin' my, dig-gin' my grave.

Dig-gin' my, dig-gin' my, dig-gin' my, dig-gin' my, dig-gin' my, dig-gin' my,

dig-gin' my, dig-gin' my, dig-gin' my grave.

ALWAYS REMEMBER US THIS WAY

Words and Music by
LADY GAGA, NATALIE HEMBY,
HILLARY LINDSEY and LORI McKENNA

Moderately slow folk rock ♩ = 66

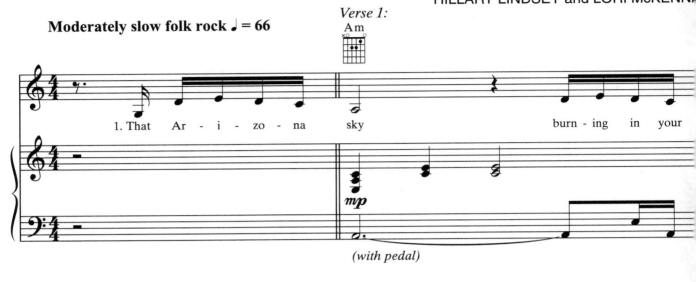

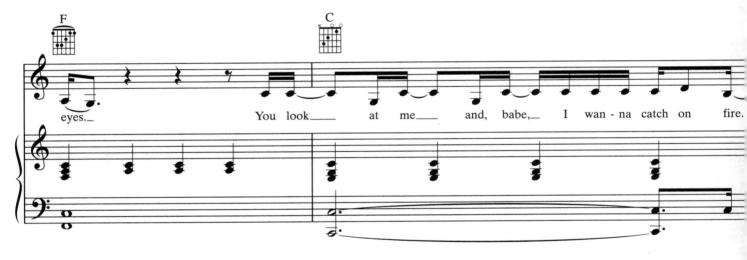

Always Remember Us This Way - 6 - 1

46

Verse 2:

F G C F G
band won't play, I'll al - ways re - mem - ber us
Am F G Am
this way, whoa, yeah. When you look at me and the
mf
F G C F G
whole world fades, I'll al - ways re - mem - ber us this way.
Freely
N.C.
mp
rit.
F B♭ F C
Hoo hmm ha hmm.

LOOK WHAT I FOUND

Words and Music by
LADY GAGA, PAUL BLAIR,
NICK MONSON, LUKAS NELSON,
MARK NILAN JR. and AARON RAITIERE

Look What I Found - 5 - 1

51

look What I Found - 5 - 2

56

HEAL ME

Heal Me - 6 - 1

Chorus:

I DON'T KNOW WHAT LOVE IS

Words and Music by
LADY GAGA and LUKAS NELSON

Slowly ♩ = 63

I don't know what love is_____ if I can't have you here. I can't know what love is._____

66

IS THAT ALRIGHT?

Words and Music by
LADY GAGA, PAUL BLAIR,
NICK MONSON, LUKAS NELSON,
MARK NILAN JR. and AARON RAITIERE

Is That Alright? - 5 - 1

68

Is That Alright? - 5 - 3

WHY DID YOU DO THAT?

Words and Music by
LADY GAGA, DIANE WARREN
PAUL BLAIR, NICK MONSON
and MARK NILAN JR.

Why Did You Do That? - 8 - 1

76

HAIR BODY FACE

Words and Music by
LADY GAGA, PAUL BLAIR,
NICK MONSON and MARK NILAN JR

Hair Body Face - 8 - 1

82

Hair Body Face - 8 - 3

84

TOO FAR GONE

Words and Music
BRADLEY COOPER and LUKAS NELSON

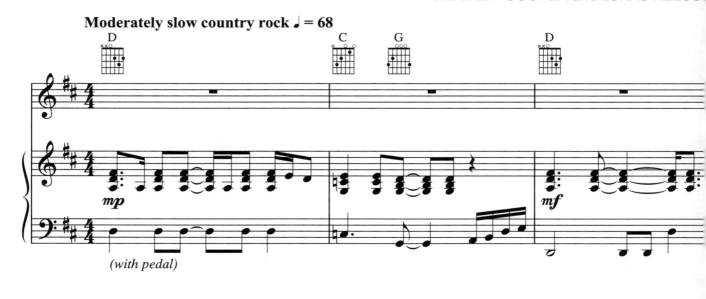

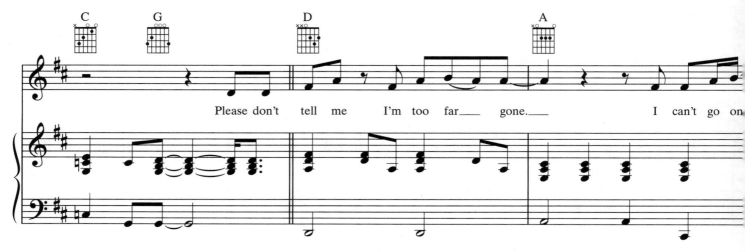

Please don't tell me I'm too far___ gone.___ I can't go on

___ if I ain't liv-in' in your arms.___ Please don't tell me I'm too far___ gone.

Too Far Gone - 2 - 1

I'LL NEVER LOVE AGAIN

Words and Music by
LADY GAGA, NATALIE HEMBY,
HILLARY LINDSEY and AARON RAITIERE

I Never Love Again - 8 - 2

92

I'll Never Love Again - 8 - 3

Verse 2:

met, I nev-er thought that I would fall,___ I nev-er thought that I'd

find my-self___ ly - in' in your arms.___ And I

wan-na pre-tend_ that it's not true, oh, ba - by, that you're gone. 'Cause my

world keeps turn-ing and turn-ing and turn-ing,___ and I'm not mov-in' on. Don't wan-na feel an-oth-er

ll Never Love Again - 8 - 4

94

I'll Never Love Again - 8 - 5

Bridge:

I don't wan-na know this feel - ing un - less it's you__ and me.___

I don't wan-na waste a mo - ment, ooh._____

And I don't wan-na give some-bod-y else the bet - ter part_ of me.___

I would rath-er wait for you,__ ooh._____ Don't wan-na

96

Chorus:

G(9)　　　　　　　　　　　　　　　　　Em7(4)

feel an-oth-er touch,　　don't wan-na start an-oth-er　fi　-　re.　　　　Don't wan-na know an-oth-er

Cmaj13　　　　　　　　　　　　　　　　Am7/D

kiss,　　　　ba - by, un - less they　are＿　your＿ lips.　　Don't wan - na give my heart a

G(9)　　　　　　　　　　　　　　　　　Em7(4)

way＿＿＿＿＿　to an - oth - er　stran - ger　　or let an - oth - er day be -

Cmaj13　　　　　　　　　　　Am7/D　　　　　　　　　　G(9)

gin.　Won't e - ven let the sun - shine＿　in.　　Oh, I'll＿　nev-er love＿　a - gain,

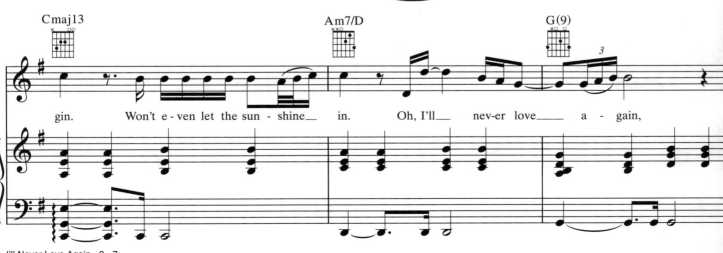

I'll Never Love Again - 8 - 7

BEFORE I CRY

Words and Music by
LADY GAGA, PAUL BLAIR,
NICK MONSON and MARK NILAN JR

Before I Cry - 5 - 1